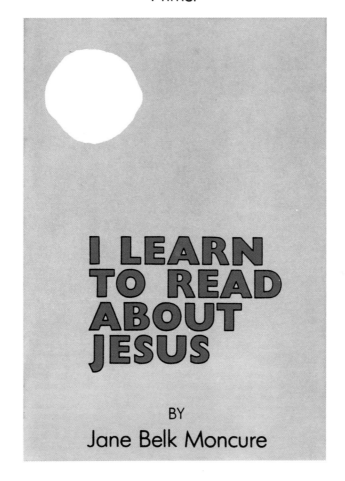

I LEARN TO READ ABOUT JESUS

BY

Jane Belk Moncure

STANDARD PUBLISHING
Cincinnati, Ohio
2950

Illustrators:

Kathryn Hutton, Pages 8-27, 76-81, 92-98, 112-123
Linda Sommers Hohag, Pages 30, 31, 74, 75, 90, 91, 124, 125
Vera K. Gohman, Pages 48-73
Diana Magnuson, Pages 100-111
Robert Masheris, Pages 32-45
Frances Hook, Pages 29, 46

Cover Art by Nan Pollard

532

Prepared for Standard Publishing by The Child's World.

ISBN 0-87239-660-6

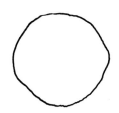

I LEARN
TO READ
ABOUT
JESUS

TABLE
OF
CONTENTS

Stories

Poems and Prayers

Also in This Book

Following A Tradition

The new Basic Bible Readers are a beautiful up-to-date edition of the famous Standard Bible Story Readers by Lillie A. Faris, that were first printed in 1925—and last revised in 1962. Millions of copies of these books have been added to the libraries of homes, schools, and churches.

The best of the former readers has been retained, including the favorite Bible stories that forever appeal to children. But the stories have been rewritten with a fresh, up-to-date approach. And all of the illustrations are new—drawn by noted children's artists of today.

Whether it's a beginning reader with his very own primer, an older child enjoying his developing reading skills, or a parent, teacher, or grandparent, we think all will heartily agree: some traditions are worth preserving!

Introduction

I Learn to Read About Jesus is a Bible primer for the beginning reader who is in the first grade. In public school the child is having the happy experience of reading for himself. Parents and Bible-school teachers should take advantage of the child's eagerness to read and provide Bible-story books that he can read for himself. This Basic Bible Primer is such a book. Although not all children learn at the same rate, an average reader will know all except the new Bible words by the end of the first semester in first grade. The number of Bible words already learned will be determined by the child's religious background.

The pictures on each page were carefully planned to introduce visually the new Bible words. The relation of pictures to words is also emphasized by the illustrated word lists at the beginning of each story. Even before the child begins to read the stories, he may learn these unfamiliar Bible words by reading the illustrated word lists with the help of an adult.

While this primer probably will be used mostly in the home, it is valuable for Christian day schools and the Bible school. Copies should be in the church library so that teachers and parents may borrow them for reference or for inspection in deciding what to buy. The teacher may place the book on the reading table for use before class or in free Bible activity time. If several copies are available, the teacher may like to have the class read together some of the stories. Or sections may be copied on a reading chart or chalkboard for the class to read together.

THE BABY JESUS

This story is about

baby Jesus

Mary

Joseph

Bethlehem

the inn

the innkeeper

a manger

a stable

a donkey

sheep and lambs

shepherds

angels

9

This is Mary.

This is Joseph.

This is Bethlehem
long ago.

Mary and Joseph
went to Bethlehem
long ago.

This is the inn in Bethlehem.

Joseph asked, "May we stay?"

This is the innkeeper
who sent them away.
Where did they go?

They went to the stable
in Bethlehem long ago.
Who was born in the stable?

Baby Jesus was born
in the stable.

These are the shepherds.

These are the sheep and lambs.

When the shepherds
were with their sheep one night,

an angel came,
and the shepherds
were afraid.

The angel said,
"Do not be afraid.
I bring you good news.

A Savior is born this day
in Bethlehem.
Go and see the baby.
Baby Jesus is the king."

Then many angels
came and praised God.
When they had gone,

the shepherds said,
"Let us go to Bethlehem
to see the baby Jesus."

The shepherds
went as fast
as they could go.

The shepherds
were so happy
to see baby Jesus, God's Son.

Then the shepherds
went away.
They told the Good News
that Jesus was born
in Bethlehem.

Today at Christmas
we tell the Good News.
Baby Jesus was born
in Bethlehem.

Sleep, baby Jesus,
    sleep in the stable.
Little lambs watch
    and shepherds pray.

Sleep, as your
    mother, Mary, holds you
safe in her arms
    this holy day.

We love You,
  baby Jesus.
We love You,
  God's own Son.
We are so glad
  You came to show
God's love for every one.

WISE-MEN COME

This story is about

the star

Wise-men

Jerusalem

gifts

King Herod

Jesus, the little king.

These are the Wise-men.

This is the star
far away.

"We will follow the star,"
the Wise-men say.

"We will find
the one who is born King!"

The Wise-men go
to Jerusalem.

"Where is the one
who is born King?" they ask.
"We saw the star."
"Where is the little King?"

"We do not know;
Go and ask King Herod."
So the Wise-men go

to see King Herod.

"Where is the little King?

We saw His star."

"Go to Bethlehem
and you will find
the little King."

So the Wise-men
go to Bethlehem.

They find Jesus,
the little King.
The Wise-men give gifts
of love to Jesus.

For they are so glad
to see God's Son!

Today, at Christmas,
we give gifts of love
as did the Wise-men
of long ago.
We give gifts,
for we are so glad
Jesus came.

THE
BOY
JESUS

This story is about

the boy Jesus

the carpenter shop

Joseph

the temple in Jerusalem

teachers

in the temple

God's Word

long ago

This is the carpenter
shop in Nazareth.

Jesus helps Joseph
in the carpenter shop.

Jesus is twelve years old.
He is going to Jerusalem.

He is going
with Mary and Joseph.

Many fathers and mothers
are going to Jerusalem.
Boys and girls are going too.

They are going to Jerusalem
for a great holy week.
They are going to the temple.
The temple is God's house.

God's Word is in God's house.
This is God's Word long ago.

This is a teacher in God's house.
The teacher reads God's Word
to the people.

Jesus talks with the teachers
in the temple.
He listens.
He learns.

Jesus stays in the temple.

He stays and stays.

He listens.

He learns.

Now the week is over.
It is time to go home.

Where is Jesus?

Mary and Joseph think that Jesus
is with the other boys and girls.
But Jesus is not.

Where is Jesus?

Mary and Joseph look for Him.

"We must find Jesus."

"We must go back to Jerusalem."

So Mary and Joseph
go back to Jerusalem.

They look one, two, three —
three days.
Where is Jesus?

Mary and Joseph
go to the temple.

They find Jesus!
He is with the teachers
in the temple.

"Son, we have been
looking for you.
Why did you stay
in the temple?"

Jesus stood up.

"God is my Father.

This is my Father's house.

I must do my Father's work."

Jesus went back to Nazareth
with Mary and Joseph.

When Jesus grew to be a man,
He did God's work.

When Jesus was a boy,
He went to God's house.
   He listened
   and learned
   of God's love.
Today, we go to
God's house too.
   We listen
   and learn
   of God's love.

JESUS AND THE BOY WHO SHARED HIS LUNCH

This story is about

Jesus

a boy

five little loaves of bread

two little fish

many hungry people

This is the boy who
shared his lunch with Jesus.

One day Jesus was teaching
about God's love.
People listened.
People learned.

People stayed near Jesus
for a long time.
They stayed past lunch.

They stayed on and on.

It was late.

The people were hungry!

"What can we give these people to eat?"
said one of Jesus' helpers.
"We have no money
to buy bread."

Then they saw a boy
with his lunch.
The boy had five loaves of bread
and two fish.

The boy gave his lunch
to Jesus.
"I will share my lunch,"
the boy said.

Jesus took the five loaves
and the two fish.
Jesus thanked the boy.
Jesus thanked God
for the boy's gift.

Then Jesus began
to break the bread
and fish into pieces.

His helpers passed
the pieces of food
to the people.

The people could hardly
believe what they saw.
There was food for every one!

And there was food left —
twelve full baskets!
"Only Jesus could do
such a great thing,"
the people said.

Jesus showed that children
can do things for God.
He said that everyone
should . . .

"Be loving."

"Be kind."

"Be honest."

"Share with others."

JESUS AND THE LITTLE SICK GIRL

This story is about

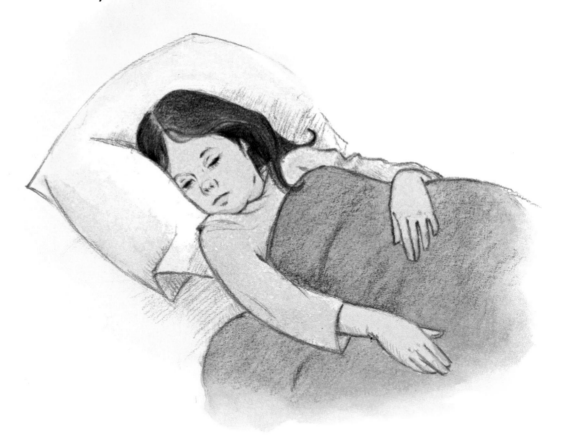

a little sick girl

Jairus, the
little girl's
father

Jesus,
who made
the girl well

One day, a little sick girl's
father, Jairus,
came to Jesus.

"Please help my little girl,"
he said. "She is dying.
But I know you
can make her well."

Jesus went to the
little girl's house.
Jesus took her hand.
"Little girl," He said, "sit up."

The little girl
opened her eyes.
Then she sat up.

Jairus was so happy!
His little girl was well again.
And Jesus had made her well!

A PRAYER

God, be with us
through every day
As we run
and skip
and play.
Keep us in Your
loving care.
Bless Your children
everywhere.
In Jesus' name.

Amen.

THE
LITTLE
LOST LAMB

This story is about

sheep
and lambs

a sheepfold

the good
shepherd

a little
lost lamb

Here are some
sheep and lambs.
How many sheep and lambs?
One hundred sheep and lambs!

This is the good shepherd.
He takes care of the
sheep and lambs.

At night the good shepherd
takes the sheep and lambs
home to the sheepfold
so they will be safe.

He counts the sheep and lambs.

He counts . . . 95 . . . 96 . . . 97 . . . 98 . . . 99 . . .

"One little lamb is not here,"

the shepherd says.

"I will go and find him."
The good shepherd
goes into the hills.

He looks for his
little lost lamb.

At last the good shepherd
finds the little lamb.
He takes the little lamb
into his arms.

He goes back to the
sheepfold.
Now all of his sheep
and lambs are safe.

Jesus said that He
is like the good shepherd.
We are like His
sheep and lambs.
Jesus said that He loves
us and will always
love us!

JESUS
AND THE
CHILDREN

This story is about

Jesus

Jesus' helpers

mothers

boys and girls

love

113

"I see Jesus; I see Him,"
said a little boy.
"I see Jesus, too,"
said a little girl.

"Please, Mother,"
begged the little boy.
"Let me talk to Jesus."
"Let me talk to Jesus, too,"
said the little girl.

"Hurry, children," said the mother.
"I will take you."

Soon, other children came too . . .
running, skipping to see Jesus.

But as they came near,
one of Jesus' helpers said,
"Stop! Jesus does not have
time to see the children."

The mother was sad
to hear this.
"I want the children
to see Jesus," she said.

The children were sad too.
They turned away.

But Jesus saw them and
said to His helpers,
"Let the children come to me."

Jesus took the children
into His arms and blessed them
that happy day long ago.
So, it is true. It is true.
Jesus loves the little children.
He always will.

*Jesus loves the
little children . . .
All the children of
the world.
Red, brown, yellow . . .*

black and white,
they are precious in His sight.
Jesus loves the
little children of the world.

New Basic Bible Vocabulary

This book contains a total of 270 words. One-hundred-ninety-six of these words should be familiar to first-grade children. They are found either on the *EDL Reading Vocabulary List* or the *Macmillan Basic Vocabulary List.* Both lists were formulated from evaluations of basal reading series.

Listed below are the additional words introduced in this Primer. These are either Bible words or words necessary for telling the Bible stories. Many first-grade children will be familiar with them — from their Sunday-school material or Bible storybooks. Children may need help in decoding proper names and places.

The words for *Jesus Loves the Little Children* are exempt from vocabulary control.

8. Bethlehem
   inn
   innkeeper
   Jesus
   Joseph
   Mary
9. angels
   donkey
   manger
   shepherds
   stable
10. Mary
11. Joseph
12. Bethlehem
13. Bethlehem
    Joseph
    Mary
14. Bethlehem
    inn
    Joseph
15. innkeeper
    sent
16. Bethlehem
    born

stable
17. born
    Jesus
    stable
18. shepherd
20. shepherds
21. afraid
    angel
    shepherds
22. afraid
    angel
23. Bethlehem
    born
    Jesus
    Savior
24. angels
    God
    praised
25. Bethlehem
    Jesus
    shepherds
26. shepherds
27. God's
    Jesus

shepherds
Son
28. Bethlehem
    born
    Jesus
    shepherds
29. Bethlehem
    born
    Christmas
    Jesus
30. arms
    holy
    Jesus
    Mary
    pray
    shepherds
    stable
31. God's
    Jesus
    own
    Son
32. Jerusalem
    Wise-men
33. gifts

Herod
Jesus
34. Wise-men
36. follow
    Wise-men
37. born
38. Jerusalem
    Wise-men
39. born
40. Herod
41. Herod
    Wise-men
42. Bethlehem
43. Bethlehem
    Wise-men
44. gifts
    Jesus
    Wise-men
45. God's
    Son
47. Christmas
    gifts
    Jesus
    Wise-men

48. carpenter
Jesus
Joseph
Nazareth

49. God's
Jerusalem
temple

50. carpenter
Nazareth

51. carpenter
Jesus
Joseph

52. Jerusalem
Jesus
twelve

53. Joseph
Mary

54. Jerusalem

55. God's
Jerusalem
temple

56. God's

57. God's

58. Jesus
learns
listens
temple

59. Jesus
learns
listens
temple

60. week

62. Jesus
Joseph
Mary

63. Jesus
Joseph
Mary

64. Jerusalem
Jesus

65. Jerusalem
Joseph
Mary

66. Jesus

67. Joseph
Mary
temple

68. Jesus
temple

69. Son
temple

71. God
Jesus
stood

72. Jesus
Joseph
Mary
Nazareth

73. God's
Jesus

74. God's
Jesus
learn
learned

listen
listened

76. bread
Jesus
loaves

78. Jesus
shared

79. God's
Jesus
learned
listened
teaching

80. Jesus
past

81. hungry
late

82. bread
Jesus'

83. bread
loaves

84. Jesus
share

85. gift
God
Jesus
loaves

86. bread
break
Jesus
pieces

87. helpers
passed

pieces

88. believe
food
hardly

89. food
full
Jesus
left

89. such
twelve

90. God
Jesus
loving

91. honest
share

92. sick

93. Jairus
Jesus

94. Jairus
Jesus
sick

95. dying

96. Jesus

98. Jairus
Jesus

99. Amen
bless
God
Jesus'
loving
skip
through

101. sheepfold
shepherd

102. hundred

103. shepherd

104. safe
sheepfold
shepherd

105. counts
shepherd

106. goes
shepherd

108. arms
shepherd

109. goes
safe
sheepfold

111. Jesus
shepherd

112. Jesus

113. Jesus'

114. Jesus

115. begged
Jesus

117. Jesus
skipping

118. Jesus
Jesus'

119. Jesus

121. Jesus

122. arms
blessed
Jesus
true

Basic Word List

Following is a list of the basic words used in this book. They are found on the *EDL Reading Vocabulary List* or the *Macmillan Basic Vocabulary List*.

a	children	grew	last	old	small	today
about	close	had	let	on	so	told
again	come	hand	like	one	some	too
ago	could	happy	little	only	soon	took
all	day	have	long	opened	star	turned
always	did	he	look	other	stay	two
an	do	hear	looking	over	stayed	up
and	does	help	lost	people	stop	us
are	eat	her	love	play	story	very
as	every	here	lunch	please	takes	want
ask	everywhere	hills	made	prayer	talk	was
asked	eyes	him	make	read	teachers	watch
at	far	his	man	run	tell	we
away	fast	holds	many	running	thanked	well
baby	fathers	home	may	sad	that	went
back	find	house	me	said	the	were
baskets	fish	how	money	sat	their	what
be	five	hurry	mother	saw	them	when
been	for	I	must	say	then	where
began	girl	in	my	see	there	who
boy	girl's	into	name	she	these	why
bring	give	is	near	sheep	they	will
but	glad	it	news	shop	thing	with
buy	go	keep	night	should	think	word
by	going	kind	no	show	this	work
came	gone	King	not	showed	three	years
can	good	know	now	sit	time	you
care	great	lamb	of	sleep	to	your